Introduction
by Claire & Julie

Do you need some fresh ideas? Then this is the book for you. We have brought together a variety of designs for you to try out, interpret or adapt. Whether you're a beginner or a seasoned professional, we know you'll find inspiration between the covers of this book.

When we approached artists to help with *Illusion and Friends*, we were overwhelmed by their generosity and enthusiasm. In this, the first in the *Illusion Step-by-Step* series, we have 30 designs from 24 different artists. They range from humorous to horror, animal to abstract and pretty to playful.

Each stunning step-by-step features a completely original piece of art that has been created especially for this book. If you find a particular style you like, many of our artists have included details of their websites so you can see more of their work.

Our easy-to-follow photographic stages are presented with clear written instructions. There are plenty of three-minute faces as well as some more elaborate designs, making *Illusion and Friends* the ideal companion on a professional job but also invaluable for anyone wanting to paint for the first time.

With the publication of this book, we are delighted to build on the success of *Illusion*, now the foremost magazine for today's face and body artist. This book continues the vision of the magazine in uniting artists from all over the world in an exchange of creative ideas.

26

36

38

Our heartfelt thanks all the artists involved in this project. We hope you enjoy the book

Claire & Julie

42

See our website for details and how to subscribe to Illusion, which is published three times a year: www.illusionmagazine.co.uk. Feel free to offer feedback about Illusion and Friends and let us know of any step-by-step designs or artists you would like to see featured in our next book.

Contents

52

54

60

61

Royal Puppy
by Jodi Carr

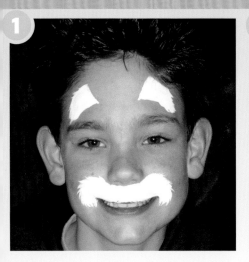

1

Paint two white ears on the forehead and a fluffy white moustache on the upper lip.

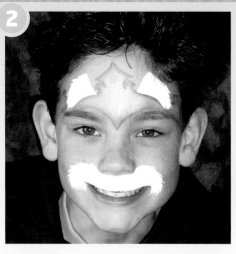

2

Sitting over the ears, add the crown in gold. Outline in brown, blending into the gold.

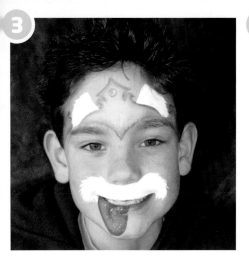

3

Paint a green stone with white highlight in the centre of the crown. With pink, paint a tongue to one side of lower lip extending part way down the chin. Outline and texture the tongue with red and highlight with white.

4

Shade the inside of your floppy ears with pale blue and outline the entire design in black. Add some black dots and shading to the muzzle. Use black to paint the ball of the nose and accent with a white highlight. Fetch, Your Highness!

Note: To make a princess puppy add blush to the cheeks and create a more feminine crown with extra pretty jewels and some swirls.

Model: Louise **Photographer:** Brian Oliver
Website: www.myfunkyfaces.co.uk

Sizzling Snake
by Julie Oliver

On one cheek, paint the basic shape of the snake's neck, head and mouth in green.

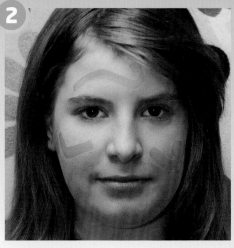

Still in green, paint a 'V' shape on the other cheek. Across the forehead paint the end of the tail, finishing in a slight ball.

On the top of the snake add highlights in yellow. Underneath add a shadow in dark blue. Paint a blue hat and shade with purple.

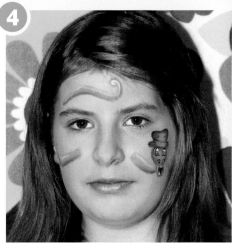

Now with a fine brush, start to add the detail. Paint the eyes in white. Add green irises and outline in black. Add nostrils and eyebrows. Highlight these in white. Add the mouth in a dark pink and don't forget the fangs!

5

Add white dots to the body of the snake and highlight the hat. In black, outline the face, hat and body. Outline the white dots. Add black semi-circles at the end of each section of the snake to act as holes for the snake to wiggle through. To create a 3D effect, shade with a mid-tone brown. Charmed, I'm sure!

Model: Jasmine **Photographer:** Chris Pick
Website: www.picktorial.co.uk

Cheeky Cheetah
by Claire Pick

1

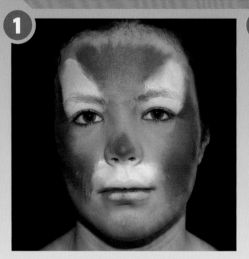

Sponge white over the eyelids, above the eyes and over and above the top lip. Add yellow down the centre of the face and across the cheeks. Add orange to the forehead and cheeks, and blend inwards into the yellow. Also paint the end of the nose orange.

2

With black on a number 4 brush, paint hair round the edge of the white eye area and make a nose. Create a muzzle, dot in whisker holes and add whiskers.

3

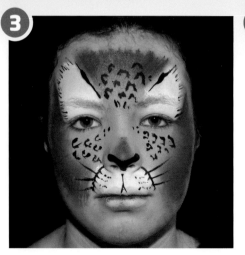

Now use your brush to paint black irregular horseshoe shapes radiating out from between the eyes and across the cheeks to create the cheetah spots.

4

Finish each of the spots with a dot of gold and white. With fine black and gold strokes, add more hair around the edge of the face. Paint the lower lip with gold.

5 Add a touch of glitter to the bottom lip and around the edge of the face. Roaaar!

Model: Livvy Simons **Website:** www.justforfunproductions.nl

Carnival Clown
by Josje Wolters

1

Apply white paint around the mouth and the eyes using a brush. Work with the natural shape of the cheek.

2

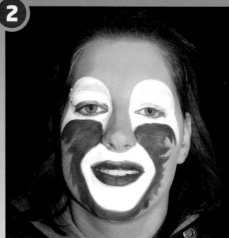

Brush on red around the white of the mouth and under the eyes.

3

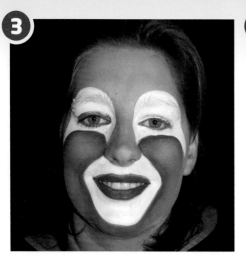

Apply yellow on the cheeks and blend into the red with a sponge.

4

Edge the white above and to the sides of the eyes with turquoise and then green. Make a red dot on the top of the nose. Paint some different coloured balloons with fine black strings on the cheeks and forehead. Apply satin powder to the cheeks and red nose.

5 Finish with white dots on the green eyebrows, a light spot on the balloons and the tip of the nose, a black line under the eyes, and a black mark on the chin. Roll up, roll up, come to the show!

Model: Ellie-Louise Edworthy **Website:** www.aface4u.co.nz

Garden Princess
by Emma Edworthy

1

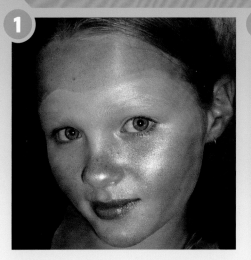

Sponge the face with shimmer white. Add light blue around the eyes and edges of the face towards the jaw line.

2

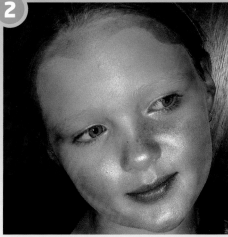

With a sponge apply an outside line of slightly darker blue, blending together and moving up to the forehead. Add a small amount of purple either side of the eyes.

3

Double load your brush with white/blue and then white/purple to make petals, forming flowers of different sizes.

4

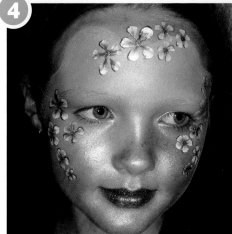

Create shadows by outlining some of the petals with a little black. Add gold to the middle of the flowers and the lips.

5 Paint a very thin line around the lips and blend in. Finish with some white dots and glitter to add to the royal garden party.

Model: Jason Urbanski Website: www.myspace.com/NPWolfe

White Tiger
by Nick Wolfe

Sponge in the shape of a tiger's head in white.

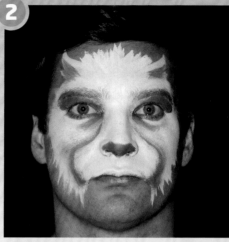

Mix in a little black to get a dark grey on your sponge. Use this to shade in ears, eyes and around the nostrils and mouth.

Using a size 3 round brush, paint on evil eyebrows and outline the nose, ears and mouth in black.

Still using black, outline the face using thin to thick lines. Start the stripes and dot in the whisker holes. Paint the lips and add some curved triangles for the teeth.

Finish the stripes then clean your brush and load it up with white. Paint thin whiskers and highlight the fangs. You'll put the grrr in tiger, baby!

Mardi Gras
by Christina Davison

1

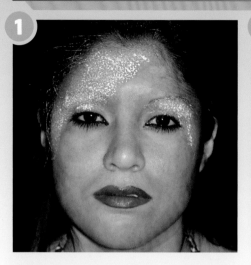

Sponge a mauve base around the eyes, forehead and into the hairline. Using light blue and white, stipple some texture onto this background colour.

2

On top of your base, create an abstract pattern with dark purple. Use the shape of the face, curls, or your model's clothing for inspiration.

3

This design works best if it is asymmetrical.

4

Decorate with swirls and dots of bright white to put some bling on your base. Strategically placed teardrops and strings of graduated dots add a feminine touch. Paint the lips purple.

5 For the final touch use black to add some accents and shadows along the lower edges of your design and to outline and shade the lips. Get ready to Samba!

Blue Butterfly
by Glyn Goodwin

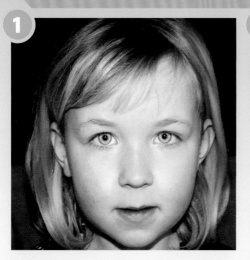

Load a damp sponge with two blues, one on each edge. With the lighter blue, swipe the sponge across each eye to create two triangular shapes.

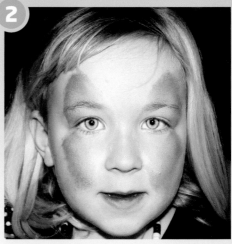

Sponge the darker blue around the outside edge of your shapes and blend the two colours together.

Using a size 6 round brush paint the outline of the wings in black. While it is still wet, drag the paint inwards using a rake brush.

Dab a blue head and body along the nose and paint in some black antennae. Paint the lips shades of blue with a black edging and blend together.

5 Edge the wings with white and use white dots to add a symmetrical pattern. Your transformation is complete – you can spread your wings!

Dragon Mask
by Des Shupe

1

Sponge dark blue over the eyebrows and eyelids. Use a lighter blue to give the lower edges a batwing shape and fade up into the dark blue.

2

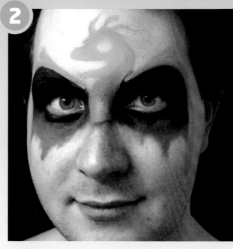

With light blue on your brush create the head and back of the dragon's neck and edge the wings. Using light green, paint the crest and the underside of the neck.

3

Paint in the eye using yellow. Also with yellow add some scales down the dragon's neck, highlight the outer edges of the crest, and paint some claws around the wings. Fill in the mouth with pink and red.

4

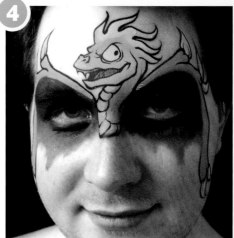

Outline the head and wings in black. Take care to keep your hand steady and your lines thin as you add character details around the eye and mouth. Give your dragon some teeth.

5

Finish outlining the mask in black. Use white to highlight the crest, face, claws and arms, and to fill in the pointy teeth. Go back in with some light blue to highlight the bottom edge of the wing. Now, where's that princess?!

Tropical Eyes
by Lorna Strachan

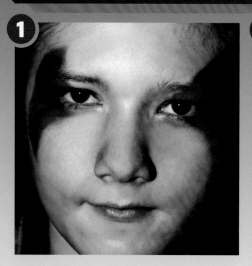

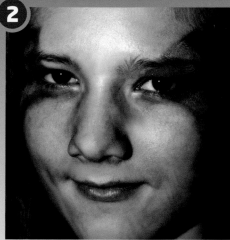

Apply pink base colour in triangular shapes at the outer edge of each eye. Take care to follow the eye shape. Apply blue to break the base colour.

On top of these two colours, apply yellow. This can be quickly and roughly applied without blending.

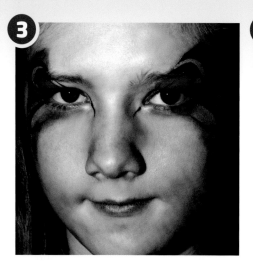

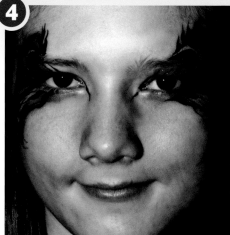

Over the colour, begin to pick up the eye shape with black highlights.

Complete the black line work by integrating finer brush strokes, particularly at the upper edges, taking care to encompass all of the base colours.

5 Paint the lips with pink and blend edges with blue. Add white dots to highlight the pattern. Alternatively highlights can be in UV or neon; for the adult/nightclub market, this whole face can be done in UV colours. Sizzlin'!

Model: Nia Lue **Photographer:** Luximages
Website: www.fabaic.com

Princess of Hearts
by Marcela Murad

Apply a little blush on the cheeks and pale blue eye shadow to the eyelids. Paint a red heart in the middle of the forehead.

Paint two small pale blue flowers on either side of the heart. Add another on each corner of the eye. With yellow, create three teardrops at the tip of the heart.

Paint a small red heart underneath each of the flowers at the edge of the eye. Add a few leaves of greenery alongside each flower.

With white, paint some highlights on the hearts and flowers, and a string of pearls into the hairline.

5 Edge and shadow the design with a little black. Colour the lips in pink. Aah, what a cutie!

Terrific Tiger
by Tiana Tong

1

Sponge white on the upper lip area and around the eyes in triangular shapes. Sponge orange over the rest of the face from the hairline to just below the cheekbones with orange.

2

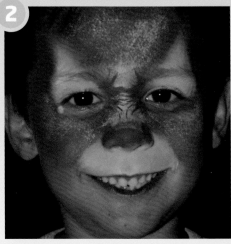

Get your model to scrunch up their eyes and nose to create natural angry lines while you stipple yellow over the bridge of the nose. Also stipple over the apples of the cheeks and middle of the forehead.

3

With black fill in natural lines created from stippling on the nose. Continue with the black to line the eyes and paint thin-to-thick-to-thin lines on the forehead, making sure to evenly space the lines. This face should be symmetrical.

4

Still with black, paint the nose and connect it with a line to the middle of the lip. Trace the smile lines to just past the tip of the nose to make a muzzle. On each side of the muzzle paint three stripes of connecting dots tapering in a downwards curve. Fill in the lips.

5

Again with black, make dots of varying sizes tapering from the inner corner of the eye ending around mid cheekbone. Continue the dots into lines to frame the face and create stripes. Follow the lines of the muzzle for the downward stripes and the lines of the cheekbones for the stripes going up past the eyes. A few yellow dots placed symmetrically in some of the thicker stripes will add highlights. Add white fangs for a terrrific finish!

Teddy Bear
by Cathy Corbett

1

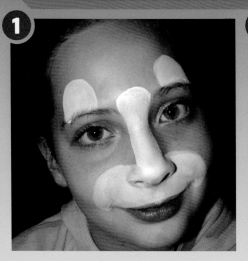

Sponge white down the centre of the nose, over the eyebrows and above the lip to create a muzzle.

2

Sponge a pink wavy line around the eyes and fill around the eyes and over the cheeks.

3

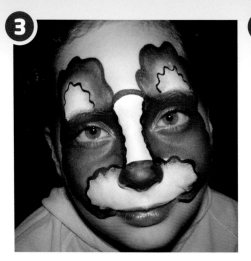

Outline the shapes you have created with black and use a rake brush to drag the black into the colour. Paint the end of the nose in black.

4

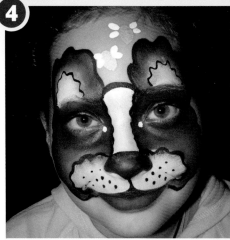

On the forehead paint a couple of yellow oval shapes for the bees. Add white wings. With a small amount of black on a sponge, rub around the eyes. Using a brush, paint black dots on the muzzle and colour the lips orange.

5 Finish the bees by outlining in black and adding stripes, heads and antennae. Also outline the lips with the black. Now where's the honey?

Enchanted Fairy
by Mandy Lawrence

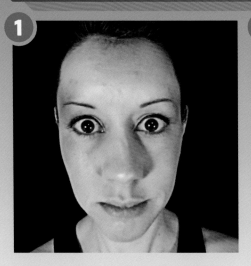

Sponge a base of pink on the forehead and top of the cheekbones. Line the top lids with black and lightly cover the eyelids with pink. Sweeping up into the hairline, sponge purple in the centre of the forehead and across the eyes.

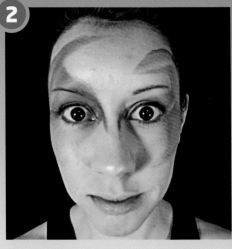

With dark green on your brush, paint around the eye and cheek area in an asymmetric design. Highlight with yellow, blending to create a lighter green too.

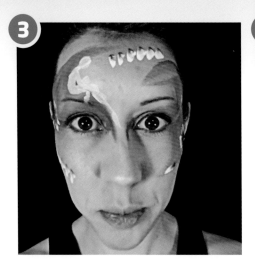

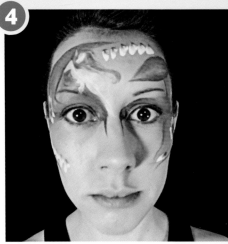

Load a size 4 round brush with white to paint the shape of the fairy nestling on one of the leaves. Double load your brush with blue/white to make the lily of the valley flowers hanging down from the leaf shapes you have created.

Outline the leaves with a darker green. Paint in the fairy's flowing hair in brown and add a dress in pink.

5 Paint in some white fairy wings. Using black, outline the fairy and add facial features. Add some white highlights and black shadows to her hair. Continue to outline the design in black, shadowing the flowers and leaves to add dimension. Paint the lips a mid-blue, lined and blended with dark green. Magic!

Metal Menace
by Sharon Hodges

Sponge a base of silver paint in the shape of a mask.

Use dark grey to outline the mask, filling in the eye sockets, lips and centre of the forehead and chin. Use this paint to create robotic-style lowlights and symmetrical metallic panels.

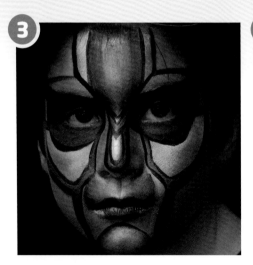

Outline your pattern in black.

Add a circle of red to the centre of the forehead and chin. Edge these in dark grey and paint in a rectangle on the bottom lip to house the teeth.

5 Paint in the teeth in white and grey. Use the white to add some subtle highlights and you've got yourself a real mean machine!

Barbed Beauty
by Cree Dykins

1

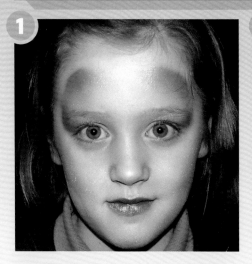

Sponge a base of sparkle white all over. To highlight eyelids, cheekbones and forehead, sponge on dark grey blended with electric black and then, with a finger, dab over iridescent white.

2

Paint a red heart in the middle of the forehead and outline it with black, shading the sides slightly. Add light reflection with white.

3

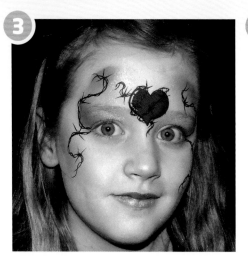

With black on your brush create barbed-wire shapes from the corners of the eyes up to the forehead and down to the cheeks. Wrap some around the heart.

4

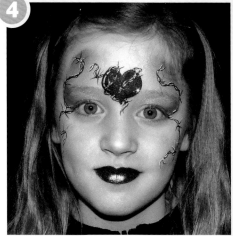

Paint the lips red with a little black blended from the edges. Add a touch of iridescent white in the centre of the bottom lip. Using a fine liner brush add white highlights to the barbed wire. Add a bright flare on the heart and a touch of glitter.

Pretty Parrot
by Des Shupe

1

To start the face, use white to paint a circle shape just shy of the centre of the forehead, and block in where the beak will go. With red, working back from the top of the head, begin to fill in the parrot's body, wings and tail.

2

Paint in some wing and tail feathers, first with blue, then with yellow. Blend these colours back into the red a bit, but do not blend them together. They should appear as separate feathers.

3

With yellow, colour the beak from the chin forward, blending into the white to make a nice creamy colour. Using grey, paint in the parrot's four-toed feet and the lower part of the beak. Shade a little around where the eye will go and give the bird a rosy cheek for character.

4

Outline the parrot in black with a small brush. Flicking the brush outward every so often will help give the bird a feathered look.

5 Fill in the iris of the eye with green and then use white to add highlights to your parrot. Who's a pretty Polly?

Camouflage Skull
by Sean Avram

1

Sponge half of the face with a base of lime green.

2

Still using a sponge, stipple a complementary darker shade of green mainly around the eye, along the nose, across the cheek and at the edges of the lighter base.

3

With a round brush, start the black line work. An oval on the cheeks is the key to creating a believable jaw line and protruding cheekbone. Make the painted jaws shorter than the actual jaw to create a foreshortening effect. Use a dry sponge to pull some black down onto the jawbone.

4

Highlight the shadows using white on a round brush. Use single teardrop strokes to create the teeth. The secret is to load the brush up, start with the middle teeth and work out to the molars. The teeth will appear naturally shaded as the paint runs out.

5

To make the teeth look scary, use black on a round brush to paint in cracks and long stress lines. Also add cracks and holes and a few dots to age the skull. With brown or copper add some cracks to the human side of the face. To make the skull appear to float, fill in under the jawbone with black for maximum scariness!

Model: Kim Tas **Photographer:** Famke Backx
Website: www.colours-grime.nl

Spring Flowers
by Saskia de Wit

1

Sponge on a yellow base, moving diagonally from the forehead across the whole nose and mouth.

2

Sponge the other side of the face with orange, dabbing over the edge into the yellow to create a smooth border.

3

With flowing brush strokes paint three big white flowers with long thin petals.

4

Add some simple curls with green for the leaves.

Add a red dot to the centre of each flower and apply red to the lips. Add white shimmer paint and a touch of glitter over the flowers to complete the design. Voilà, spring has sprung!

Dreamcatcher
by Catriona Finlayson-Wilkins

1

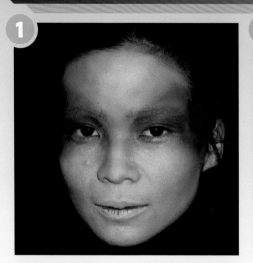

Sponge a blue base onto the face. Try a teal colour in the middle with sparkle blue edges for a good combination. Darken the area around the eyes with navy and a hint of purple. Blend into the other blues.

2

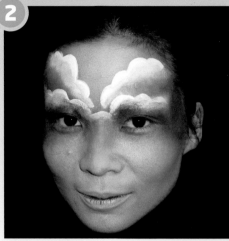

With a size 5 round brush, paint a series of white 'M' shapes as the upper outline of clouds. Drag-blend this down into the blue. Start with the highest layer of clouds, leaving a little blue showing at the bottom of that cloud before painting the white line for the next.

3

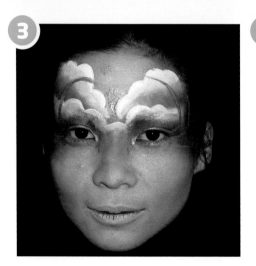

Popping out between the clouds, add a gold semi-circle. Brush three gold lines, curved upwards like radiating spokes from the outer eye corners. One line follows the upper eyelid, before curling up to form a semi-circle over the sun. For shimmer, rub a little pearl white onto the cloud.

4

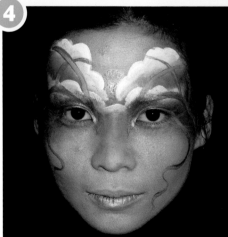

Repeat the curved spokes in the opposite direction so they criss-cross the original lines. Taper and wiggle the ends. Paint the bottom lip gold.

5 Add small yellow and hot pink dots with white highlights to the gold lines. Add some small white stars and dots to the night sky and finish with glitter. Now your rising sun is all set to destroy the bad dreams trapped by your golden web!

April Showers
by Lorna Strachan

Sponge pink base around the eyes, forehead and cheekbones.

Sponge blue around the edges of the pink base. Take particular care to blend into the eyelids, and have a clear break from the temple to the corner of the eye. This has the effect of opening the eyes.

Using a one stroke rainbow, start to highlight the face shape with line work. The edges need not be crisp.

Start to edge the rainbows with different sized white teardrop shapes. Use the smallest ones on the inner edges of the eye and down the nose.

 5 Finish with a few clusters of fine white dots following the face and rainbow shapes. Shade the lips and apply rainbow highlights. With a little practice, this is a vibrant three-minute face.

Big Cat Mask
by Brian Wolfe

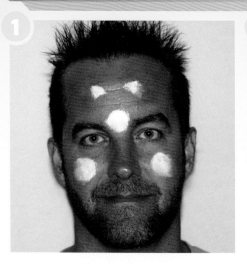

Sponge a white circle on each cheek and between the eyebrows. Add two triangles to make the ears.

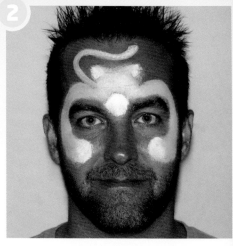

With yellow, sponge two leg shapes to wrap round the model's eyes, and a face under the white ears. Use a brush to paint a tail extending onto the forehead.

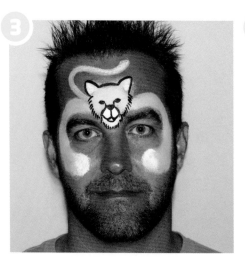

Using black on a number 2 round brush, outline the head. Paint in a heart-shaped nose, split lip, and eyes with black running down the sides of the muzzle.

Continue to outline the legs, tail and paws in black. Add some claws, whisker holes and face detail.

5 Add black spots and white highlights to the eyes and claws. White whiskers and a pink mouth complete the mask. Watch out, you've been spotted!

Horse Play
by Christina Davison

1 On one side of the face roughly outline the shape of a horse's face in brown paint. Starting between the eyebrows and going all the way down to the upper lip, paint a wide white stripe down the nose.

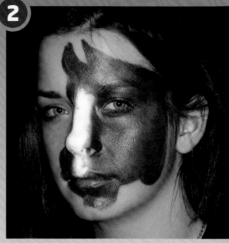

2 Fill in the shape with a metallic brown, which gives the appearance of horsehair.

3 Outline the horse's head and ears with black or dark brown.

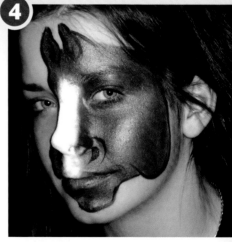

4 Add in the nostrils and a little shading on the cheekbone and jaw line, and around the ears and eye sockets.

5 Use dark brown to paint in a fluffy mane between the ears and on top of the head. For models with long hair you can paint into the hairline so their own hair becomes part of the mane. Giddy up!

Otter
by Katrina Bate

1

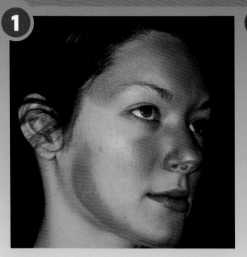

Sponge shimmer grey brown over the forehead, across the cheekbones and bridge of the nose, and along the jaw line.

2

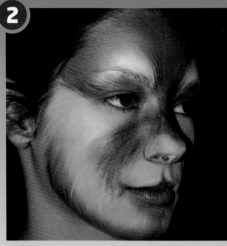

With the edge of the sponge apply white to the other areas in a sweeping motion to give a slightly furry effect.

3

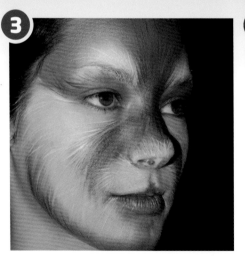

Using a dagger brush begin to build up the fur using alternate darker browns and white.

4

Outline the muzzle with dark grey and dot the base ready for whiskers. Apply black on the end of the nose. In a slightly downward motion with a dagger brush, sweep whiskers over the cheeks.

5 Apply black glitter to the nose. A dab of pink glitter lip gloss will put the finishing touch on this cute furry friend.

Model: Lonneke Warnier **Photographer:** Famke Backx
Website: www.colours-grime.nl

Fantasy Eyes
by Saskia de Wit

Sponge a perfect circle of pearl white to the whole of the face. Sponge a little pink around the circle and blend together.

With a brush, paint a mask in leaf-like shapes around each eye in purple. Make the designs similar but not symmetrical.

Use a small round brush to paint thin lines around the mask in darker purple, blending as you go. Line and paint the lips in a similar fashion.

Paint curls from the tips of some of the leaf-like shapes. Add lots of dots, following the flow of the curls and leaves.

5 Purple shimmer powder or loose glitter applied to the mask will add a finishing touch of glamour!

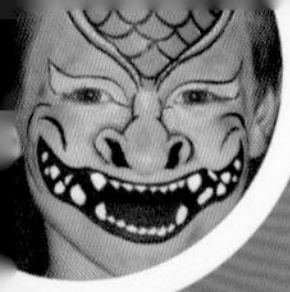

Model: Christopher Beeks Website: www.facepainting4u.co.uk

Monster Mouth

by Tammy Beeks

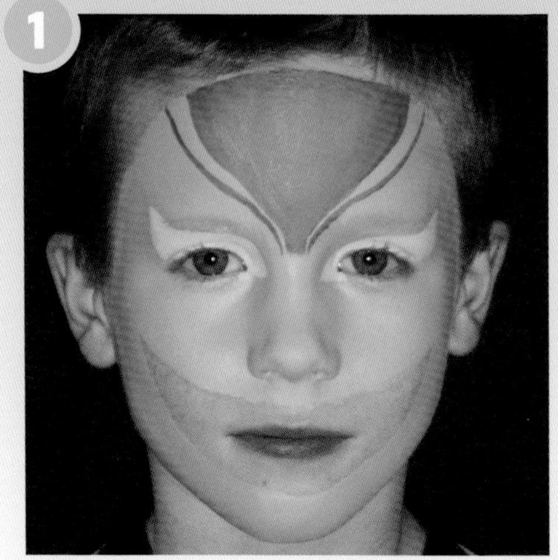

Sponge an even base of mid-green over the face, leaving the mouth area clear. Brush a dark green triangle on the forehead with a thin line on either side. Paint the eyelids with lime green, flicking up on either side.

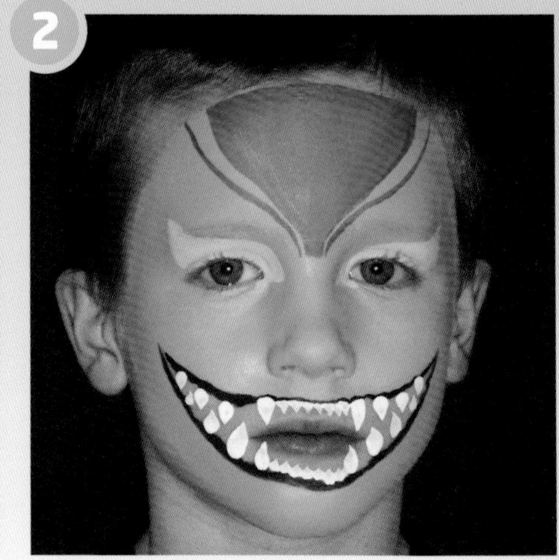

Outline the extra large mouth in red. Paint in white teeth of various shapes and sizes.

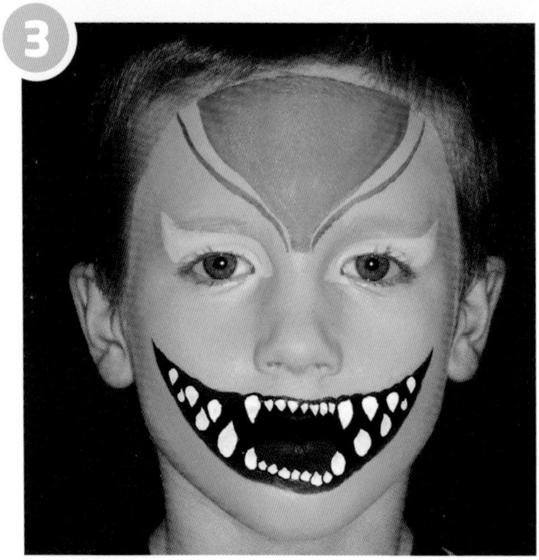

Fill in between the teeth with black, leaving an area for the tongue on and under the bottom lip. Add the tongue in red and paint a thin black line down the middle.

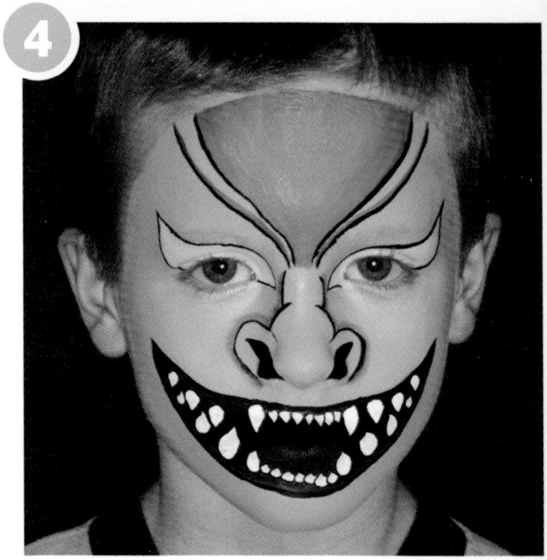

Outline the lips, eyelids and triangle in black. Create a nose with black, adding large nostrils. Shade with light brown to create shadows.

5 Sparsely load a sponge with dark green and stipple over the cheeks, chin, nose and eyebrows. Paint black scales in the triangle. Add some smile lines on the cheeks around the mouth. With white highlight the scales and cheeks, and add small dots around the eyes and on the forehead. Watch out, there's a monster about!

Floral Fun
by Sharon Hodges

1

Sponge a base over one eye and down the side of the face with shimmer paint, and apply dark pink to the eyelids.

2

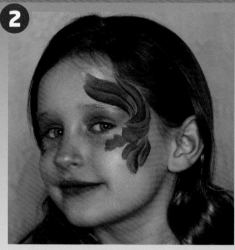

Tip a brush with white and then use pink to make bold strokes in a descending pattern over the shimmer paint. Make a much smaller accent next to the other eye.

3

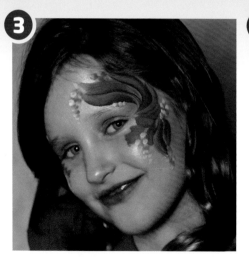

Double load a round brush with green and white to add some greenery around the pink in short flowing grape-like patterns.

4

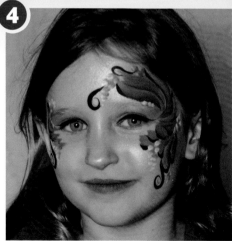

Outline some of your swirls with black. Add a few decorative twists and curls, and outline the upper eyelids.

5

Colour the lips pink and add some graduated white dots to highlight the design. Floral fun for all!

Flaming Skull
by Dawn Perry

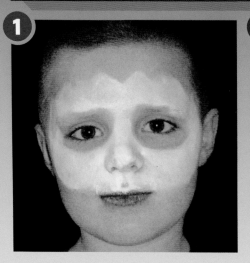

Sponge in the shape of a skull in white. Around the edges, where the flames will go, sponge yellow over the white.

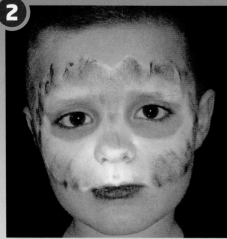

Blending outwards, sponge over orange and then red.

Use a size 6 or 8 round brush to paint a black mask around the eye sockets. Also paint the nose, cheeks and lips black.

Define the flames around the face in red or dark pink size 3 or 4 round brush.

5 Outline the whole face in black. With a size 2 round brush create broken teeth and fangs in the white area above and to the sides of the lips. Fangstastic!

Silver Petal Princess
by Zoë Thornbury-Phillips

1

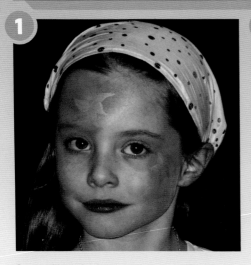

Sponge a blend of pink and mauve over one side of the forehead, over the opposite cheek and both eyelids. Paint the first layer of your silver flowers, one in each area.

2

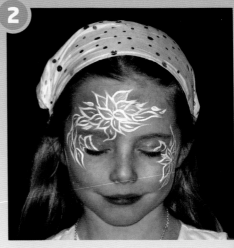

Build up the flowers in layers. With silver, outline each petal from the centre and as you reach the tip lift your brush up gently, away from the face with a flick, causing a point to form. Fill in with silver and then outline each petal in white. Take some of the petals over the eyelids.

3

Add pink dots to the centre of each flower. Add some purple and pink paint to the lips.

4

To finish add dark purple shadows to each petal and complete with glitter. Petal perfect!

Masquerade
by Tiana Tong

1

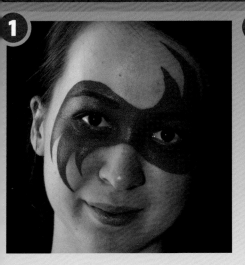

Create your mask by painting a pink base in an 'S' shape around the eyes. Stipple with metallic colour.

2

Outline the edges in purple, a shade darker than the pink, and drag blend into the base colour with a dry brush.

3

Outline with black and drag blend into the purple. Line eyes with a design to mirror and complement the outline shape.

4

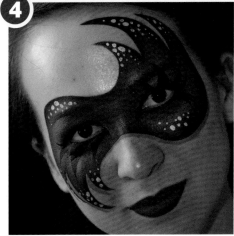

Add lipstick in pink lined with purple. Accent the mask with dots of gold. Line the bottom of the mask with light brown mixed with some blue to create a shadow. You shall go to the ball!

Meet The Artists

Jodi Carr

Julie Oliver

Claire Pick

Josje Wolters

Emma Edworthy

Nick Wolfe

Christina Davison

Glyn Goodwin

Des Shupe

Lorna Strachan

Marcela Murad

Tiana Tong